50 Sweet and Savory Delights Recipes

By: Kelly Johnson

Table of Contents

- Chocolate Chip Cookies
- Cinnamon Rolls
- Lemon Poppy Seed Muffins
- Peach Cobbler
- Apple Cinnamon Streusel Bread
- Raspberry Lemon Cheesecake Bars
- Classic Banana Bread
- Carrot Cake Cupcakes with Cream Cheese Frosting
- Chocolate Lava Cakes
- Salted Caramel Brownies
- Red Velvet Cake
- Churros with Chocolate Dipping Sauce
- Almond Joy Energy Bites
- Buttermilk Pancakes
- French Toast Casserole
- Strawberry Shortcake
- Blueberry Lemon Scones

- Pecan Pie Bars
- S'mores Cupcakes
- Chocolate Eclairs
- Lemon Bars
- Key Lime Pie
- Apple Crisp
- Gingerbread Cookies
- Nutella-Stuffed Crepes
- Spinach and Feta Stuffed Croissants
- Caprese Salad
- Stuffed Mushrooms
- Bacon-Wrapped Dates
- Cheesy Garlic Breadsticks
- Potato Skins
- Mozzarella Sticks
- Sweet and Sour Meatballs
- Chicken Parmesan Bites
- Spinach Artichoke Dip
- Mini Quiches

- Guacamole with Tortilla Chips
- Jalapeño Poppers
- BBQ Chicken Sliders
- Loaded Nachos
- Pulled Pork Sliders
- Hummus with Pita Chips
- Parmesan Roasted Potatoes
- Beef Wellington Bites
- Shrimp Scampi
- Fried Zucchini Fries
- Buffalo Cauliflower Bites
- Stuffed Bell Peppers
- Margherita Pizza
- Chicken Caesar Salad Wraps

Chocolate Chip Cookies

Ingredients:

- 2 1/4 cups all-purpose flour
- 1/2 tsp baking soda
- 1 cup unsalted butter, room temperature
- 1/2 cup granulated sugar
- 1 cup packed brown sugar
- 1 tsp salt
- 2 tsp pure vanilla extract
- 2 large eggs
- 2 cups semisweet chocolate chips

Instructions:

1. Preheat the oven to 350°F (175°C). Line baking sheets with parchment paper.
2. In a bowl, whisk together flour and baking soda. Set aside.
3. In a large mixing bowl, beat the butter, granulated sugar, brown sugar, and salt until smooth and creamy.
4. Add the vanilla extract and eggs, one at a time, mixing well after each addition.
5. Gradually add the dry ingredients to the wet ingredients, mixing until combined.
6. Fold in the chocolate chips.

7. Drop rounded tablespoons of dough onto the prepared baking sheets, spacing them about 2 inches apart.

8. Bake for 10-12 minutes or until the edges are golden brown.

9. Let the cookies cool on the baking sheets for a few minutes before transferring them to a wire rack to cool completely.

Cinnamon Rolls

Ingredients:

- 1 cup warm milk (110°F/45°C)
- 2 1/4 tsp active dry yeast
- 1/2 cup granulated sugar
- 1/2 cup unsalted butter, melted
- 2 large eggs
- 4 cups all-purpose flour
- 1 tsp salt
- 1/2 cup brown sugar, packed
- 2 tbsp ground cinnamon
- 1/4 cup unsalted butter, softened
- 1 cup powdered sugar
- 1 tsp vanilla extract
- 2 tbsp milk (for glaze)

Instructions:

1. In a small bowl, combine warm milk, yeast, and sugar. Let it sit for about 5 minutes until it becomes frothy.

2. In a large bowl, combine flour and salt. Add the yeast mixture, melted butter, and eggs. Mix until a dough forms.

3. Knead the dough on a lightly floured surface for about 5-7 minutes until smooth. Place the dough in a greased bowl, cover with a towel, and let it rise for about 1-2 hours or until doubled in size.

4. Preheat the oven to 375°F (190°C).

5. Punch down the dough and roll it into a rectangle about 12x18 inches.

6. Spread softened butter over the dough, then sprinkle with brown sugar and cinnamon.

7. Roll the dough up tightly, then cut it into 12 even slices.

8. Place the rolls in a greased baking dish and bake for 20-25 minutes or until golden brown.

9. In a small bowl, mix powdered sugar, vanilla extract, and milk to make the glaze.

10. Drizzle the glaze over the warm cinnamon rolls before serving.

Lemon Poppy Seed Muffins

Ingredients:

- 1 1/2 cups all-purpose flour
- 1 tsp baking powder
- 1/2 tsp baking soda
- 1/4 tsp salt
- 1/4 cup poppy seeds
- 1/2 cup unsalted butter, room temperature
- 3/4 cup granulated sugar
- 2 large eggs
- 1 tsp vanilla extract
- Zest of 1 lemon
- 1/4 cup fresh lemon juice
- 1/2 cup sour cream

Instructions:

1. Preheat the oven to 375°F (190°C). Line a muffin tin with paper liners.
2. In a bowl, whisk together flour, baking powder, baking soda, salt, and poppy seeds.
3. In a separate large bowl, cream together the butter and sugar until light and fluffy.

4. Add the eggs one at a time, mixing well after each addition. Stir in the vanilla extract, lemon zest, and lemon juice.

5. Gradually add the dry ingredients to the wet ingredients, alternating with sour cream. Mix until just combined.

6. Divide the batter evenly among the muffin cups.

7. Bake for 18-20 minutes or until a toothpick inserted into the center comes out clean.

8. Let the muffins cool in the tin for 5 minutes before transferring to a wire rack to cool completely.

Peach Cobbler

Ingredients:

- 4 cups fresh or frozen peaches, peeled and sliced
- 1/2 cup granulated sugar
- 1 tbsp cornstarch
- 1/2 tsp ground cinnamon
- 1/4 tsp ground nutmeg
- 1 tbsp lemon juice
- 1 1/2 cups all-purpose flour
- 1/4 cup granulated sugar
- 2 tsp baking powder
- 1/2 tsp salt
- 1/4 cup unsalted butter, melted
- 1/2 cup milk
- 1 tsp vanilla extract

Instructions:

1. Preheat the oven to 375°F (190°C).
2. In a large bowl, combine the peaches, sugar, cornstarch, cinnamon, nutmeg, and lemon juice. Stir until the peaches are evenly coated.
3. Pour the peach mixture into a greased 9x9-inch baking dish.

4. In another bowl, combine flour, sugar, baking powder, and salt. Add the melted butter, milk, and vanilla extract. Stir until just combined.

5. Spoon the batter over the peaches, spreading it evenly.

6. Bake for 40-45 minutes or until the topping is golden brown and the peach filling is bubbling.

7. Let the cobbler cool for a few minutes before serving. Optionally, serve with vanilla ice cream or whipped cream.

Apple Cinnamon Streusel Bread

Ingredients:

- **For the bread:**
    - 2 cups all-purpose flour
    - 1 tsp baking soda
    - 1/2 tsp ground cinnamon
    - 1/4 tsp salt
    - 1/2 cup unsalted butter, room temperature
    - 1 cup granulated sugar
    - 2 large eggs
    - 1 tsp vanilla extract
    - 1/2 cup sour cream
    - 1 1/2 cups peeled, chopped apples (such as Granny Smith)
- **For the streusel topping:**
    - 1/2 cup all-purpose flour
    - 1/2 cup brown sugar, packed
    - 1/4 tsp ground cinnamon
    - 1/4 cup unsalted butter, cubed

Instructions:

1. Preheat oven to 350°F (175°C). Grease a loaf pan.

2. In a medium bowl, whisk together flour, baking soda, cinnamon, and salt.

3. In a large bowl, beat together butter and sugar until light and fluffy. Add eggs one at a time, then vanilla extract.

4. Add the dry ingredients, alternating with sour cream. Stir in the chopped apples.

5. For the streusel topping, combine flour, brown sugar, cinnamon, and cubed butter. Use a fork or pastry cutter to blend until crumbly.

6. Pour the batter into the prepared loaf pan and sprinkle with the streusel topping.

7. Bake for 55-60 minutes or until a toothpick inserted into the center comes out clean.

8. Let cool before serving.

Raspberry Lemon Cheesecake Bars

Ingredients:

- **For the crust:**
  - 1 1/2 cups graham cracker crumbs
  - 1/4 cup granulated sugar
  - 1/2 cup unsalted butter, melted

- **For the cheesecake filling:**
  - 3 (8 oz) packages cream cheese, softened
  - 1 cup granulated sugar
  - 3 large eggs
  - 1 tsp vanilla extract
  - Zest and juice of 1 lemon
  - 1/2 cup raspberry jam or fresh raspberries

Instructions:

1. Preheat oven to 325°F (160°C). Line an 8x8-inch baking pan with parchment paper.

2. For the crust: Mix graham cracker crumbs, sugar, and melted butter. Press into the bottom of the prepared pan.

3. For the filling: Beat cream cheese and sugar until smooth. Add eggs one at a time, mixing well. Add vanilla, lemon zest, and lemon juice.

4. Pour the filling over the crust and drop spoonfuls of raspberry jam over the top. Use a toothpick to swirl the jam into the filling.

5. Bake for 30-35 minutes until set. Let cool completely, then refrigerate for at least 2 hours before cutting into squares.

Classic Banana Bread

Ingredients:

- 1 3/4 cups all-purpose flour
- 1 tsp baking soda
- 1/4 tsp salt
- 1/2 cup unsalted butter, softened
- 1 cup granulated sugar
- 2 large eggs
- 4 ripe bananas, mashed
- 1 tsp vanilla extract
- 1/2 cup buttermilk or milk

Instructions:

1. Preheat oven to 350°F (175°C). Grease a loaf pan.
2. In a bowl, whisk together flour, baking soda, and salt.
3. In a separate large bowl, cream together butter and sugar. Add eggs one at a time, then bananas and vanilla extract.
4. Gradually mix in the dry ingredients, alternating with milk, until just combined.
5. Pour the batter into the prepared loaf pan and bake for 60-65 minutes or until a toothpick comes out clean.
6. Let cool before slicing.

Carrot Cake Cupcakes with Cream Cheese Frosting

Ingredients:

- **For the cupcakes:**

    - 1 1/2 cups all-purpose flour

    - 1 1/2 tsp baking powder

    - 1/2 tsp baking soda

    - 1 tsp ground cinnamon

    - 1/4 tsp ground nutmeg

    - 1/4 tsp salt

    - 1/2 cup vegetable oil

    - 1 cup granulated sugar

    - 2 large eggs

    - 1 1/2 cups finely grated carrots

    - 1/2 cup chopped walnuts or raisins (optional)

- **For the frosting:**

    - 8 oz cream cheese, softened

    - 1/4 cup unsalted butter, softened

    - 2 cups powdered sugar

    - 1 tsp vanilla extract

Instructions:

1. Preheat oven to 350°F (175°C). Line a muffin tin with paper liners.

2. In a bowl, whisk together flour, baking powder, baking soda, cinnamon, nutmeg, and salt.

3. In another bowl, mix oil, sugar, and eggs. Stir in grated carrots and walnuts/raisins.

4. Gradually add dry ingredients to the wet mixture. Divide batter evenly into cupcake liners.

5. Bake for 18-20 minutes or until a toothpick comes out clean. Let cool completely.

6. For the frosting: Beat cream cheese and butter until smooth. Gradually add powdered sugar and vanilla, then frost the cooled cupcakes.

Chocolate Lava Cakes

Ingredients:

- 1/2 cup unsalted butter
- 6 oz semisweet chocolate, chopped
- 1 cup powdered sugar
- 2 large eggs
- 2 large egg yolks
- 1 tsp vanilla extract
- 1/4 cup all-purpose flour
- Pinch of salt

Instructions:

1. Preheat oven to 425°F (220°C). Grease 4 ramekins and place on a baking sheet.
2. Melt butter and chocolate in a microwave-safe bowl or using a double boiler. Stir until smooth.
3. Whisk in powdered sugar, then eggs, egg yolks, vanilla, flour, and salt.
4. Divide the batter evenly between ramekins.
5. Bake for 12-14 minutes until the edges are set but the center is soft.
6. Let cool for 1-2 minutes, then invert onto plates and serve warm.

Salted Caramel Brownies

Ingredients:

- **For the brownies:**
    - 1/2 cup unsalted butter
    - 1 cup granulated sugar
    - 1/4 cup unsweetened cocoa powder
    - 2 large eggs
    - 1 tsp vanilla extract
    - 1/2 cup all-purpose flour
    - 1/4 tsp salt

- **For the caramel:**
    - 1/2 cup unsalted butter
    - 1 cup packed brown sugar
    - 1/4 cup heavy cream
    - 1 tsp vanilla extract
    - 1/2 tsp sea salt

Instructions:

1. Preheat oven to 350°F (175°C). Grease a 9x9-inch baking pan.

2. For the brownies: Melt butter and mix with sugar and cocoa. Add eggs and vanilla, then stir in flour and salt.

3. Pour batter into the pan and bake for 20-25 minutes, or until a toothpick comes out clean.

4. For the caramel: In a saucepan, melt butter, then stir in brown sugar, cream, and vanilla. Bring to a simmer for 3-4 minutes, then remove from heat and stir in sea salt.

5. Pour caramel over the cooled brownies and refrigerate for 1-2 hours to set.

Red Velvet Cake

Ingredients:

- 2 1/2 cups all-purpose flour
- 1 1/2 tsp baking powder
- 1 tsp baking soda
- 1 tsp salt
- 1 tbsp cocoa powder
- 1 1/2 cups vegetable oil
- 1 1/2 cups granulated sugar
- 2 large eggs
- 1 oz red food coloring
- 1 tsp vanilla extract
- 1 tsp white vinegar
- 1 cup buttermilk
- **For the cream cheese frosting:**
    - 8 oz cream cheese, softened
    - 1/2 cup unsalted butter, softened
    - 4 cups powdered sugar
    - 1 tsp vanilla extract

Instructions:

1. Preheat oven to 350°F (175°C). Grease and flour two 9-inch round cake pans.

2. In a bowl, whisk together flour, baking powder, baking soda, salt, and cocoa powder.

3. In a separate bowl, beat oil and sugar until smooth. Add eggs, food coloring, vanilla, and vinegar. Mix in the flour mixture, alternating with buttermilk.

4. Divide the batter between the pans and bake for 30-35 minutes, or until a toothpick comes out clean.

5. Let the cakes cool completely, then frost with cream cheese frosting.

Churros with Chocolate Dipping Sauce

Ingredients:

- 1 cup water
- 1/2 cup unsalted butter
- 1 tbsp granulated sugar
- 1/4 tsp salt
- 1 cup all-purpose flour
- 3 large eggs
- Vegetable oil for frying
- 1/2 cup granulated sugar (for coating)
- 1 tsp ground cinnamon
- **For the chocolate sauce:**
    - 1/2 cup heavy cream
    - 1/2 cup semisweet chocolate chips
    - 1 tbsp honey

Instructions:

1. In a saucepan, combine water, butter, sugar, and salt. Bring to a boil. Stir in flour and cook until the dough forms a ball.
2. Remove from heat and beat in eggs one at a time.

3. Heat oil in a deep pan for frying. Fill a piping bag with dough and pipe churros into the oil, cutting them to desired lengths.

4. Fry for 2-3 minutes until golden, then roll in a cinnamon-sugar mixture.

5. For the chocolate sauce: Heat cream in a saucepan until simmering. Pour over chocolate chips and stir until smooth. Add honey and mix.

6. Serve churros with chocolate dipping sauce.

Almond Joy Energy Bites

Ingredients:

- 1 cup rolled oats
- 1/2 cup shredded unsweetened coconut
- 1/4 cup almond butter
- 2 tbsp honey
- 1/4 cup mini chocolate chips
- 1/4 cup whole almonds

Instructions:

1. In a bowl, combine oats, coconut, almond butter, honey, and chocolate chips.
2. Roll the mixture into small balls and place an almond inside each bite.
3. Refrigerate for 30 minutes to set. Store in an airtight container.

Buttermilk Pancakes

Ingredients:

- 2 cups all-purpose flour
- 2 tbsp granulated sugar
- 2 tsp baking powder
- 1/2 tsp baking soda
- 1/2 tsp salt
- 2 large eggs
- 2 cups buttermilk
- 1/4 cup unsalted butter, melted
- 1 tsp vanilla extract

Instructions:

1. In a large bowl, whisk together flour, sugar, baking powder, baking soda, and salt.
2. In a separate bowl, beat eggs, buttermilk, melted butter, and vanilla.
3. Pour wet ingredients into dry ingredients and stir until just combined.
4. Heat a griddle or skillet over medium heat and lightly grease.
5. Pour batter onto the skillet and cook until bubbles form. Flip and cook until golden brown.
6. Serve with maple syrup and butter.

French Toast Casserole

Ingredients:

- 1 loaf day-old French bread, cut into cubes
- 8 large eggs
- 2 cups milk
- 1/2 cup heavy cream
- 1/2 cup granulated sugar
- 1 tsp vanilla extract
- 1 tsp ground cinnamon
- 1/2 tsp salt
- 1/4 cup unsalted butter, melted
- 1/4 cup maple syrup (for drizzling)

Instructions:

1. Preheat oven to 350°F (175°C). Grease a 9x13-inch baking dish.
2. Place bread cubes in the dish.
3. In a bowl, whisk together eggs, milk, cream, sugar, vanilla, cinnamon, and salt. Pour over the bread cubes and gently press to soak the bread.
4. Drizzle melted butter over the top.
5. Bake for 45-50 minutes until the top is golden and a toothpick comes out clean.
6. Drizzle with maple syrup and serve warm.

Strawberry Shortcake

Ingredients:

- **For the shortcakes:**
    - 2 cups all-purpose flour
    - 1/4 cup granulated sugar
    - 1 tbsp baking powder
    - 1/2 tsp salt
    - 1/2 cup unsalted butter, cold and cubed
    - 3/4 cup heavy cream
    - 1 tsp vanilla extract

- **For the filling:**
    - 4 cups fresh strawberries, hulled and sliced
    - 2 tbsp granulated sugar
    - 1 cup heavy cream
    - 2 tbsp powdered sugar
    - 1 tsp vanilla extract

Instructions:

1. Preheat oven to 400°F (200°C). Grease a baking sheet.

2. For the shortcakes: In a bowl, combine flour, sugar, baking powder, and salt. Cut in the cold butter until the mixture resembles coarse crumbs. Stir in cream and

vanilla until dough forms.

3. Drop spoonfuls of dough onto the baking sheet and bake for 12-15 minutes or until golden brown.

4. For the filling: Toss strawberries with sugar and let sit for 10 minutes. Whip cream with powdered sugar and vanilla until stiff peaks form.

5. Slice shortcakes in half and top with strawberries and whipped cream.

Blueberry Lemon Scones

Ingredients:

- 2 cups all-purpose flour
- 1/4 cup granulated sugar
- 1 tbsp baking powder
- 1/2 tsp salt
- 1/2 cup unsalted butter, cold and cubed
- 1 cup fresh blueberries
- 1 tbsp lemon zest
- 1/2 cup heavy cream
- 1 large egg
- 1 tsp vanilla extract
- 1 tbsp milk (for brushing)
- 1 tbsp coarse sugar (for topping)

Instructions:

1. Preheat oven to 400°F (200°C). Line a baking sheet with parchment paper.
2. In a large bowl, combine flour, sugar, baking powder, and salt. Cut in butter until the mixture resembles coarse crumbs.
3. Gently fold in blueberries and lemon zest.

4. In a separate bowl, whisk together cream, egg, and vanilla. Add to the dry ingredients and stir until just combined.

5. Turn the dough onto a floured surface and pat it into a circle. Cut into 8 wedges and place on the baking sheet.

6. Brush with milk and sprinkle with coarse sugar.

7. Bake for 18-20 minutes until golden brown.

Pecan Pie Bars

Ingredients:

- **For the crust:**
    - 1 1/2 cups all-purpose flour
    - 1/4 cup granulated sugar
    - 1/2 tsp salt
    - 1/2 cup unsalted butter, softened
- **For the filling:**
    - 1 cup corn syrup
    - 1 cup packed brown sugar
    - 1/4 cup unsalted butter, melted
    - 3 large eggs
    - 1 1/2 cups chopped pecans
    - 1 tsp vanilla extract
    - 1/4 tsp salt

Instructions:

1. Preheat oven to 350°F (175°C). Grease a 9x13-inch baking dish.
2. For the crust: In a bowl, combine flour, sugar, and salt. Cut in butter until the mixture resembles coarse crumbs. Press into the bottom of the prepared pan and bake for 15 minutes.

3. For the filling: In a bowl, whisk together corn syrup, brown sugar, melted butter, eggs, vanilla, and salt. Stir in pecans.

4. Pour the filling over the partially baked crust and bake for an additional 25-30 minutes until the filling is set.

5. Let cool completely before slicing into bars.

S'mores Cupcakes

Ingredients:

- **For the cupcakes:**
    - 1 box chocolate cake mix (or homemade)
    - 1/2 cup water
    - 1/2 cup vegetable oil
    - 3 large eggs
    - 1 tsp vanilla extract

- **For the frosting:**
    - 1 cup unsalted butter, softened
    - 3 cups powdered sugar
    - 2 tbsp heavy cream
    - 1 tsp vanilla extract
    - 1/2 cup marshmallow fluff

- **For the topping:**
    - 1/2 cup crushed graham crackers
    - 1/2 cup mini marshmallows
    - 1/2 cup chocolate chips

Instructions:

1. Preheat oven to 350°F (175°C). Line a muffin tin with cupcake liners.

2. Prepare the cake mix according to package instructions and bake for 18-22 minutes or until a toothpick comes out clean. Let cool completely.

3. For the frosting: Beat butter until creamy, then add powdered sugar, heavy cream, vanilla, and marshmallow fluff. Beat until smooth and fluffy.

4. Frost the cooled cupcakes with the marshmallow frosting, then sprinkle with graham cracker crumbs, mini marshmallows, and chocolate chips.

Chocolate Eclairs

Ingredients:

- **For the choux pastry:**
    - 1 cup water
    - 1/2 cup unsalted butter
    - 1 cup all-purpose flour
    - 1/4 tsp salt
    - 4 large eggs
- **For the filling:**
    - 2 cups heavy cream
    - 2 tbsp powdered sugar
    - 1 tsp vanilla extract
- **For the chocolate glaze:**
    - 1/2 cup heavy cream
    - 4 oz semisweet chocolate, chopped

Instructions:

1. Preheat oven to 400°F (200°C). Line a baking sheet with parchment paper.
2. For the choux pastry: In a saucepan, bring water and butter to a boil. Stir in flour and salt until smooth, then remove from heat. Add eggs one at a time, beating until smooth.

3. Pipe the dough into long eclair shapes on the baking sheet and bake for 20-25 minutes until puffed and golden.

4. For the filling: Whip cream with powdered sugar and vanilla until stiff peaks form.

5. For the glaze: Heat cream until simmering, then pour over chocolate. Stir until smooth.

6. Once the eclairs are cooled, slice them open and fill with whipped cream. Dip the tops in the chocolate glaze.

Lemon Bars

Ingredients:

- **For the crust:**
  - 1 1/2 cups all-purpose flour
  - 1/2 cup powdered sugar
  - 1/2 tsp salt
  - 1/2 cup unsalted butter, softened

- **For the filling:**
  - 4 large eggs
  - 1 1/2 cups granulated sugar
  - 1/4 cup all-purpose flour
  - 1/4 tsp salt
  - 1/2 cup freshly squeezed lemon juice
  - Zest of 1 lemon

Instructions:

1. Preheat oven to 350°F (175°C). Grease an 8x8-inch baking dish.

2. For the crust: Mix flour, powdered sugar, and salt. Cut in butter until the mixture forms a dough. Press into the bottom of the prepared pan and bake for 15-18 minutes until lightly golden.

3. For the filling: Whisk together eggs, sugar, flour, salt, lemon juice, and zest. Pour over the baked crust.

4. Bake for an additional 20-25 minutes until the filling is set.

5. Let cool, then dust with powdered sugar and slice into bars.

Key Lime Pie

Ingredients:

- **For the crust:**
    - 1 1/2 cups graham cracker crumbs
    - 1/4 cup granulated sugar
    - 1/2 cup unsalted butter, melted
- **For the filling:**
    - 3 large egg yolks
    - 1 can (14 oz) sweetened condensed milk
    - 1/2 cup freshly squeezed lime juice
    - Zest of 1 lime

Instructions:

1. Preheat oven to 350°F (175°C). Grease a 9-inch pie pan.
2. For the crust: Mix graham cracker crumbs, sugar, and melted butter. Press into the bottom of the pie pan and bake for 8-10 minutes until golden.
3. For the filling: Whisk together egg yolks, condensed milk, lime juice, and zest. Pour into the cooled crust.
4. Bake for 15-18 minutes until set. Let cool, then refrigerate for at least 2 hours before serving.

Apple Crisp

Ingredients:

- 5 cups apples, peeled and sliced
- 1 tbsp lemon juice
- 1/2 cup granulated sugar
- 1/2 tsp cinnamon
- 1/4 tsp salt
- **For the topping:**
    - 1/2 cup old-fashioned oats
    - 1/2 cup all-purpose flour
    - 1/4 cup packed brown sugar
    - 1/4 cup unsalted butter, cold and cubed

Instructions:

1. Preheat oven to 350°F (175°C). Grease a baking dish.
2. Toss apples with lemon juice, sugar, cinnamon, and salt. Spread in the prepared dish.
3. For the topping: Mix oats, flour, brown sugar, and butter. Use a pastry cutter to blend until crumbly.
4. Sprinkle the topping over the apples and bake for 40-45 minutes until golden and bubbly.

Gingerbread Cookies

Ingredients:

- 3 1/4 cups all-purpose flour
- 1 tbsp ground ginger
- 1 tbsp ground cinnamon
- 1/2 tsp ground cloves
- 1/2 tsp salt
- 1 tsp baking soda
- 1/2 cup unsalted butter, softened
- 1 cup brown sugar, packed
- 1/2 cup molasses
- 1 large egg
- 1 tsp vanilla extract

Instructions:

1. Preheat oven to 350°F (175°C). Line baking sheets with parchment paper.
2. In a bowl, whisk together flour, ginger, cinnamon, cloves, salt, and baking soda.
3. In a separate bowl, beat butter and brown sugar until creamy. Add molasses, egg, and vanilla and mix.
4. Gradually stir in dry ingredients until a dough forms. Roll out dough and cut into shapes.

5. Bake for 8-10 minutes until firm. Let cool before decorating.

Nutella-Stuffed Crepes

Ingredients:

- **For the crepes:**
    - 1 cup all-purpose flour
    - 2 large eggs
    - 1 cup milk
    - 2 tbsp melted butter
    - 1 tbsp granulated sugar
    - 1/4 tsp salt
- **For the filling:**
    - Nutella

Instructions:

1. In a blender, combine flour, eggs, milk, melted butter, sugar, and salt. Blend until smooth.
2. Heat a non-stick skillet over medium heat. Pour in a small amount of batter and swirl to coat the pan. Cook for 1-2 minutes, then flip and cook for another 30 seconds.
3. Remove the crepe and spread Nutella on one side. Fold and serve.

Spinach and Feta Stuffed Croissants

Ingredients:

- 1 package croissant dough (8 pieces)
- 2 cups fresh spinach, chopped
- 1/2 cup crumbled feta cheese
- 1/2 cup cream cheese, softened
- 1/4 cup grated Parmesan cheese
- 1 clove garlic, minced
- 1 tbsp olive oil
- Salt and pepper to taste

Instructions:

1. Preheat oven to 375°F (190°C). Line a baking sheet with parchment paper.
2. In a skillet, heat olive oil over medium heat and sauté garlic until fragrant. Add spinach and cook until wilted. Remove from heat and allow to cool slightly.
3. In a bowl, mix together spinach, feta, cream cheese, Parmesan, salt, and pepper.
4. Roll out the croissant dough and place a spoonful of the spinach mixture in the center of each croissant. Roll up the dough to form croissants.
5. Place the croissants on the baking sheet and bake for 12-15 minutes, or until golden brown.

Caprese Salad

Ingredients:

- 2 cups fresh mozzarella balls (or 1 large ball, sliced)
- 2 cups cherry tomatoes, halved
- 1/4 cup fresh basil leaves, torn
- 2 tbsp extra virgin olive oil
- 1 tbsp balsamic vinegar
- Salt and pepper to taste

Instructions:

1. Arrange mozzarella, tomatoes, and basil on a serving platter.
2. Drizzle with olive oil and balsamic vinegar.
3. Season with salt and pepper.
4. Serve immediately or refrigerate until ready to serve.

Stuffed Mushrooms

Ingredients:

- 16 large mushroom caps, stems removed and finely chopped
- 1/2 cup cream cheese, softened
- 1/4 cup grated Parmesan cheese
- 1/4 cup breadcrumbs
- 1/4 cup garlic, minced
- 2 tbsp fresh parsley, chopped
- 1 tbsp olive oil
- Salt and pepper to taste

Instructions:

1. Preheat oven to 375°F (190°C). Grease a baking sheet.
2. In a bowl, mix together cream cheese, Parmesan, breadcrumbs, garlic, parsley, olive oil, salt, and pepper.
3. Stuff the mushroom caps with the mixture, pressing gently to fill.
4. Place stuffed mushrooms on the baking sheet and bake for 20-25 minutes, or until the mushrooms are tender and the stuffing is golden.

Bacon-Wrapped Dates

Ingredients:

- 16 pitted dates
- 8 slices of bacon, cut in half
- 1/4 cup goat cheese or cream cheese (optional)
- 1 tbsp honey (optional)

Instructions:

1. Preheat oven to 375°F (190°C). Line a baking sheet with parchment paper.
2. If using cheese, stuff each date with a small amount of goat cheese or cream cheese.
3. Wrap each date with half a slice of bacon and secure with a toothpick.
4. Arrange on the baking sheet and bake for 15-20 minutes, or until the bacon is crispy.
5. Drizzle with honey for extra flavor before serving, if desired.

Cheesy Garlic Breadsticks

Ingredients:

- 1 package pizza dough (or homemade)
- 1/4 cup unsalted butter, melted
- 3 cloves garlic, minced
- 1 cup shredded mozzarella cheese
- 1/4 cup grated Parmesan cheese
- 1/2 tsp Italian seasoning
- Salt to taste

Instructions:

1. Preheat oven to 400°F (200°C). Line a baking sheet with parchment paper.
2. Roll out the pizza dough into a rectangle and place it on the prepared baking sheet.
3. Brush melted butter over the dough, then sprinkle minced garlic, mozzarella, Parmesan, Italian seasoning, and salt.
4. Use a pizza cutter to slice the dough into sticks.
5. Bake for 12-15 minutes, or until the cheese is melted and the breadsticks are golden brown.

Potato Skins

Ingredients:

- 4 large russet potatoes
- 1/2 cup shredded cheddar cheese
- 1/4 cup sour cream
- 1/4 cup crispy bacon, crumbled
- 2 tbsp green onions, chopped
- Olive oil
- Salt and pepper to taste

Instructions:

1. Preheat oven to 400°F (200°C). Scrub potatoes clean and pierce them with a fork.
2. Bake the potatoes for 45-50 minutes, or until tender. Let cool slightly, then cut in half lengthwise.
3. Scoop out the flesh, leaving a small border. Brush the skins with olive oil and sprinkle with salt and pepper.
4. Return the skins to the oven and bake for 10-12 minutes, until crispy.
5. Fill with cheese, sour cream, bacon, and green onions. Serve hot.

Mozzarella Sticks

Ingredients:

- 12 mozzarella cheese sticks, cut in half
- 1 cup all-purpose flour
- 2 large eggs, beaten
- 1 cup breadcrumbs (preferably panko)
- 1/2 tsp garlic powder
- 1/2 tsp dried oregano
- Vegetable oil, for frying
- Marinara sauce, for dipping

Instructions:

1. Freeze the mozzarella sticks for 1 hour to help them hold their shape during frying.
2. Set up a breading station: Place flour in one bowl, beaten eggs in another, and breadcrumbs mixed with garlic powder and oregano in a third.
3. Dip each mozzarella stick first in flour, then in egg, and finally in breadcrumbs, pressing gently to coat.
4. Heat vegetable oil in a deep fryer or large skillet over medium heat.
5. Fry the mozzarella sticks in batches for 1-2 minutes, or until golden brown and crispy. Drain on paper towels.
6. Serve with marinara sauce for dipping.

Sweet and Sour Meatballs

Ingredients:

- 1 lb ground beef or turkey
- 1/2 cup breadcrumbs
- 1/4 cup grated Parmesan cheese
- 1/4 cup chopped parsley
- 1 egg
- 2 tbsp olive oil
- 1 cup sweet and sour sauce

Instructions:

1. Preheat oven to 375°F (190°C). Grease a baking sheet.
2. In a bowl, mix together ground meat, breadcrumbs, Parmesan, parsley, and egg.
3. Form into 1-inch meatballs and place on the baking sheet.
4. Bake for 20 minutes, or until cooked through.
5. While the meatballs bake, heat sweet and sour sauce in a saucepan over medium heat.
6. Once the meatballs are done, toss them in the sauce and serve.

Chicken Parmesan Bites

Ingredients:

- 2 large chicken breasts, cut into bite-sized cubes
- 1 cup breadcrumbs
- 1/2 cup grated Parmesan cheese
- 1/2 cup all-purpose flour
- 2 large eggs, beaten
- 1 cup marinara sauce
- 1/2 cup shredded mozzarella cheese
- Olive oil for frying

Instructions:

1. Preheat oven to 375°F (190°C). Grease a baking dish.
2. In a shallow bowl, combine breadcrumbs and Parmesan.
3. Dredge chicken cubes in flour, dip in egg, and coat in the breadcrumb mixture.
4. Heat olive oil in a skillet over medium heat. Fry chicken pieces until golden brown on all sides, about 5-7 minutes.
5. Place the fried chicken in the prepared baking dish, top with marinara sauce, and sprinkle with mozzarella cheese.
6. Bake for 10-12 minutes, or until the cheese is melted and bubbly.

Spinach Artichoke Dip

Ingredients:

- 1 can (14 oz) artichoke hearts, drained and chopped
- 1 package (10 oz) frozen spinach, thawed and drained
- 1 cup sour cream
- 1/2 cup mayonnaise
- 1 cup grated Parmesan cheese
- 1 cup shredded mozzarella cheese
- 1 clove garlic, minced
- Salt and pepper to taste

Instructions:

1. Preheat oven to 375°F (190°C). Grease a baking dish.
2. In a bowl, combine artichokes, spinach, sour cream, mayonnaise, Parmesan, mozzarella, garlic, salt, and pepper.
3. Spread the mixture in the prepared dish.
4. Bake for 20-25 minutes, or until bubbly and golden brown on top.
5. Serve with crackers, chips, or fresh vegetables.

Mini Quiches

Ingredients:

- 1 package refrigerated pie crusts (or homemade)
- 6 large eggs
- 1/2 cup heavy cream
- 1/2 cup shredded cheese (cheddar, Swiss, or a mix)
- 1/4 cup diced ham or cooked bacon (optional)
- 1/4 cup sautéed spinach or other veggies (optional)
- Salt and pepper to taste

Instructions:

1. Preheat oven to 375°F (190°C). Grease a mini muffin tin.
2. Roll out the pie crust and cut circles to fit the muffin tin. Press the crusts into the muffin cups.
3. In a bowl, whisk together eggs, heavy cream, cheese, salt, and pepper.
4. Add in diced ham, bacon, spinach, or any other vegetables.
5. Pour the egg mixture into each muffin cup, filling about 3/4 of the way.
6. Bake for 15-20 minutes, or until the quiches are set and slightly golden on top. Let cool before serving.

Guacamole with Tortilla Chips

Ingredients:

- 3 ripe avocados, peeled and pitted
- 1 lime, juiced
- 1/2 red onion, finely chopped
- 1 tomato, diced
- 1 jalapeño, seeded and finely chopped (optional)
- 1/4 cup fresh cilantro, chopped
- Salt and pepper to taste
- Tortilla chips for serving

Instructions:

1. In a bowl, mash the avocados with lime juice until smooth or chunky, depending on your preference.
2. Stir in the onion, tomato, jalapeño (if using), cilantro, salt, and pepper.
3. Serve immediately with tortilla chips.

Jalapeño Poppers

Ingredients:

- 12 jalapeño peppers, halved and seeded
- 8 oz cream cheese, softened
- 1 cup shredded cheddar cheese
- 1/2 cup cooked bacon, crumbled (optional)
- 1/2 tsp garlic powder
- 1/2 tsp smoked paprika
- Salt and pepper to taste
- 1 cup breadcrumbs
- Olive oil for drizzling

Instructions:

1. Preheat oven to 375°F (190°C). Line a baking sheet with parchment paper.
2. In a bowl, combine cream cheese, cheddar cheese, bacon, garlic powder, paprika, salt, and pepper.
3. Stuff each jalapeño half with the cheese mixture.
4. Dip each stuffed jalapeño into breadcrumbs and place them on the baking sheet.
5. Drizzle with olive oil and bake for 20-25 minutes, until the jalapeños are tender and the breadcrumbs are golden.

BBQ Chicken Sliders

Ingredients:

- 2 cups shredded cooked chicken
- 1/2 cup BBQ sauce
- 12 slider buns
- 1/4 cup coleslaw (optional)
- 1/4 cup pickles (optional)

Instructions:

1. Preheat oven to 350°F (175°C). Slice slider buns in half and place them on a baking sheet.
2. In a bowl, toss the shredded chicken with BBQ sauce until well-coated.
3. Spoon the BBQ chicken mixture onto the bottom halves of the buns.
4. Top with coleslaw and pickles (optional).
5. Place the top halves of the buns on and bake for 10-12 minutes, or until the buns are toasted and the sliders are heated through.

Loaded Nachos

Ingredients:

- 1 large bag tortilla chips
- 2 cups shredded cheddar cheese
- 1/2 cup black beans, drained and rinsed
- 1/2 cup diced tomatoes
- 1/4 cup jalapeño slices
- 1/4 cup green onions, chopped
- 1/4 cup sour cream
- 1/4 cup salsa
- 1/4 cup guacamole (optional)

Instructions:

1. Preheat oven to 375°F (190°C). Spread tortilla chips evenly on a baking sheet.
2. Sprinkle shredded cheese evenly over the chips.
3. Add black beans, tomatoes, jalapeños, and green onions on top.
4. Bake for 10-12 minutes, or until the cheese is melted and bubbly.
5. Top with sour cream, salsa, and guacamole before serving.

Pulled Pork Sliders

Ingredients:

- 2 cups shredded cooked pulled pork
- 1/2 cup BBQ sauce
- 12 slider buns
- 1/4 cup pickled onions (optional)
- 1/4 cup coleslaw (optional)

Instructions:

1. Preheat oven to 350°F (175°C). Slice slider buns in half and place them on a baking sheet.
2. In a bowl, mix the pulled pork with BBQ sauce.
3. Spoon the pulled pork onto the bottom halves of the buns.
4. Top with pickled onions and coleslaw (optional).
5. Place the top halves of the buns on and bake for 10-12 minutes, or until the buns are toasted and the sliders are heated through.

Hummus with Pita Chips

Ingredients:

- 1 can (15 oz) chickpeas, drained and rinsed
- 1/4 cup tahini
- 2 tbsp olive oil
- 2 tbsp lemon juice
- 1 clove garlic
- Salt to taste
- 1/2 tsp cumin (optional)
- Pita chips for serving

Instructions:

1. In a food processor, blend chickpeas, tahini, olive oil, lemon juice, garlic, salt, and cumin (optional) until smooth.
2. Taste and adjust seasoning if needed.
3. Serve with pita chips for dipping.

Parmesan Roasted Potatoes

Ingredients:

- 1 lb baby potatoes, halved
- 2 tbsp olive oil
- 1/2 cup grated Parmesan cheese
- 1 tsp garlic powder
- 1/2 tsp dried thyme
- Salt and pepper to taste

Instructions:

1. Preheat oven to 400°F (200°C). Line a baking sheet with parchment paper.
2. Toss the potatoes with olive oil, Parmesan, garlic powder, thyme, salt, and pepper.
3. Arrange the potatoes cut-side down on the baking sheet.
4. Roast for 25-30 minutes, or until the potatoes are golden and crispy.

Beef Wellington Bites

Ingredients:

- 1 lb beef tenderloin (or ground beef)
- 1 package puff pastry
- 1/4 cup pâté or mushroom duxelles (optional)
- 1 egg, beaten
- Salt and pepper to taste

Instructions:

1. Preheat oven to 400°F (200°C). Roll out the puff pastry on a lightly floured surface.
2. Cut the beef into bite-sized pieces and season with salt and pepper. Sear in a hot skillet for 2-3 minutes until browned. Allow to cool.
3. Place a small spoonful of pâté or mushroom duxelles in the center of each pastry square.
4. Place the beef on top and fold the pastry around it, sealing the edges.
5. Brush with the beaten egg and bake for 15-20 minutes, or until the pastry is golden brown.

Shrimp Scampi

Ingredients:

- 1 lb large shrimp, peeled and deveined
- 1/2 cup butter
- 4 cloves garlic, minced
- 1/2 cup white wine or chicken broth
- 1/4 tsp red pepper flakes (optional)
- 2 tbsp fresh parsley, chopped
- Salt and pepper to taste
- Cooked pasta or toasted baguette for serving

Instructions:

1. In a large skillet, melt butter over medium heat.
2. Add garlic and cook for 1-2 minutes, until fragrant.
3. Add the shrimp and cook until pink, about 3-4 minutes.
4. Pour in wine or broth, red pepper flakes (optional), salt, and pepper. Simmer for 2-3 minutes.
5. Sprinkle with fresh parsley and serve over pasta or with toasted baguette slices.

Fried Zucchini Fries

Ingredients:

- 2 medium zucchinis, sliced into fries
- 1/2 cup all-purpose flour
- 1 egg, beaten
- 1 cup breadcrumbs (preferably panko)
- 1/4 cup grated Parmesan cheese
- Salt and pepper to taste
- Vegetable oil for frying

Instructions:

1. Preheat oil in a deep fryer or large skillet over medium heat.
2. Set up a breading station: flour in one bowl, beaten egg in another, and breadcrumbs mixed with Parmesan in a third.
3. Dip each zucchini fry first in flour, then egg, and finally breadcrumbs, pressing gently to coat.
4. Fry the zucchini fries in batches for 2-3 minutes, or until golden brown.
5. Drain on paper towels and season with salt and pepper.

Buffalo Cauliflower Bites

Ingredients:

- 1 medium head of cauliflower, cut into florets
- 1 cup all-purpose flour
- 1 cup water
- 1 tsp garlic powder
- 1/2 tsp paprika
- Salt and pepper to taste
- 1 cup buffalo sauce
- 2 tbsp melted butter
- Ranch or blue cheese dressing for dipping

Instructions:

1. Preheat oven to 450°F (230°C). Line a baking sheet with parchment paper.
2. In a bowl, whisk together flour, water, garlic powder, paprika, salt, and pepper to form a batter.
3. Dip each cauliflower floret into the batter, coating evenly, then place on the prepared baking sheet.
4. Bake for 25-30 minutes, or until the cauliflower is crispy and golden.
5. While the cauliflower bakes, mix the buffalo sauce and melted butter in a separate bowl.

6. Once the cauliflower is done, toss the baked florets in the buffalo sauce mixture until well-coated.

7. Serve with ranch or blue cheese dressing for dipping.

Stuffed Bell Peppers

Ingredients:

- 4 bell peppers, tops cut off and seeds removed
- 1 lb ground beef or turkey
- 1 cup cooked rice
- 1 can (14 oz) diced tomatoes
- 1 small onion, chopped
- 1 tsp garlic powder
- 1 tsp dried oregano
- 1/2 cup shredded cheese (cheddar or mozzarella)
- Salt and pepper to taste
- Fresh parsley for garnish (optional)

Instructions:

1. Preheat oven to 375°F (190°C). Grease a baking dish.
2. In a skillet, cook the ground meat over medium heat until browned. Add the chopped onion and cook until softened.
3. Stir in the cooked rice, diced tomatoes, garlic powder, oregano, salt, and pepper. Let the mixture simmer for 5-7 minutes.
4. Stuff each bell pepper with the meat and rice mixture and place them in the prepared baking dish.
5. Top each stuffed pepper with shredded cheese.

6. Cover with foil and bake for 30 minutes. Remove the foil and bake for an additional 10-15 minutes, or until the cheese is melted and bubbly.

7. Garnish with fresh parsley and serve.

Margherita Pizza

Ingredients:

- 1 pizza dough (store-bought or homemade)
- 1/2 cup pizza sauce or marinara sauce
- 8 oz fresh mozzarella, sliced
- 1-2 ripe tomatoes, sliced
- Fresh basil leaves
- Olive oil for drizzling
- Salt and pepper to taste

Instructions:

1. Preheat oven to 475°F (245°C). Roll out the pizza dough on a floured surface to your desired thickness.
2. Place the dough on a baking sheet or pizza stone.
3. Spread a thin layer of pizza sauce over the dough, leaving a small border around the edges.
4. Arrange the fresh mozzarella slices and tomato slices on top of the sauce.
5. Season with salt and pepper, and drizzle with olive oil.
6. Bake for 10-12 minutes, or until the crust is golden and the cheese is melted and bubbly.
7. Remove from the oven and top with fresh basil leaves before serving.

Chicken Caesar Salad Wraps

Ingredients:

- 2 cups cooked chicken breast, shredded or sliced
- 1/2 cup Caesar dressing
- 4 large flour tortillas
- 2 cups romaine lettuce, chopped
- 1/2 cup shredded Parmesan cheese
- Croutons (optional)

Instructions:

1. In a bowl, toss the shredded chicken with Caesar dressing until well-coated.
2. Lay out the tortillas on a flat surface.
3. Divide the lettuce evenly between the tortillas, placing it in the center of each.
4. Top the lettuce with the chicken mixture, Parmesan cheese, and croutons (if using).
5. Roll up the tortillas, folding in the sides as you go, to form a wrap.
6. Slice the wraps in half and serve immediately.

www.ingramcontent.com/pod-product-compliance
Lightning Source LLC
LaVergne TN
LVHW081619060526
838201LV00054B/2306